CRIMINAL JUSTICE SYSTEM

CONTEMPORARY ISSUES

CRIMINAL JUSTICE SYSTEM
EDUCATION
THE ENVIRONMENT
GENDER EQUALITY
GUN CONTROL
HEALTH CARE
IMMIGRATION
JOBS AND ECONOMY
MENTAL HEALTH
POVERTY AND WELFARE
PRIVACY AND SOCIAL MEDIA
RACE RELATIONS
RELIGIOUS FREEDOM

CONTEMPORARY ISSUES

CRIMINAL JUSTICE SYSTEM

ASHLEY NICOLE

MASON CREST
PHILADELPHIA | MIAMI

MASON CREST
450 Parkway Drive, Suite D, Broomall, Pennsylvania 19008
(866) MCP-BOOK (toll-free) • www.masoncrest.com

© 2020 by Mason Crest, an imprint of National Highlights, Inc.

Printed and bound in the United States of America.

CPSIA Compliance Information: Batch #CCRI2019.
For further information, contact Mason Crest at 1-866-MCP-Book.

First printing
1 3 5 7 9 8 6 4 2

ISBN (hardback) 978-1-4222-4388-6
ISBN (series) 978-1-4222-4387-9
ISBN (ebook) 978-1-4222-7403-3

Library of Congress Cataloging-in-Publication Data
on file at the Library of Congress

Interior and cover design: Torque Advertising + Design
Production: Michelle Luke

Publisher's Note: Websites listed in this book were active at the time of publication. The publisher is not responsible for websites that have changed their address or discontinued operation since the date of publication. The publisher reviews and updates the websites each time the book is reprinted.

QR CODES AND LINKS TO THIRD-PARTY CONTENT

CONTENTS

KEY ICONS TO LOOK FOR:

Words to Understand: These words with their easy-to-understand definitions will increase the reader's understanding of the text while building vocabulary skills.

Sidebars: This boxed material within the main text allows readers to build knowledge, gain insights, explore possibilities, and broaden their perspectives by weaving together additional information to provide realistic and holistic perspectives.

Educational videos: Readers can view videos by scanning our QR codes, providing them with additional educational content to supplement the text. Examples include news coverage, moments in history, speeches, iconic sports moments, and much more!

Text-Dependent Questions: These questions send the reader back to the text for more careful attention to the evidence presented there.

Research Projects: Readers are pointed toward areas of further inquiry connected to each chapter. Suggestions are provided for projects that encourage deeper research and analysis.

Series Glossary of Key Terms: This back-of-the-book glossary contains terminology used throughout this series. Words found here increase the reader's ability to read and comprehend higher-level books and articles in this field.

WORDS TO UNDERSTAND

rehabilitation—the goal of the correctional branch to facilitate a prisoner's re-entrance to society, often with the help of education, vocational training, and psychological treatment.

jurisdiction—an area in which a government agency has power to act.

prosecutor—an attorney who conducts the criminal case against an individual or organization.

OVERVIEW AND HISTORY OF CRIMINAL JUSTICE

On October 3, 1995, over 95 million people tuned in to watch the exciting conclusion of the O.J. Simpson murder trial. Most viewers had followed the televised courtroom trial for months. Now, the "trial of the century" was over, and a Los Angeles jury would decide whether Orenthal James Simpson was innocent or guilty of charges that he had murdered his former wife, Nicole Brown Simpson, and her friend Ron Goldman.

More than a year earlier, in June of 1994, a frantic dog had led Nicole Brown's neighbors to the victim's bodies. Brown and Goldman had been stabbed and left on the walkway leading to Brown's home. When photos of the ghastly crime scene emerged, the violence on display outraged the public. Immediately, Simpson was a person of interest in the murders. While the criminal justice system got to work, popular opinion was that Simpson had murdered his ex-wife. After Simpson led police on a slow-speed car chase on live television, this opinion grew stronger.

The trial of O.J. Simpson took nine months, as the prosecution and defense unveiled their cases. Due to

At the time of his arrest in 1994, O.J. Simpson was very popular. The former NFL star had developed a successful career as a movie actor.

the intense publicity surrounding the case, the twenty-four jurors chosen to hear Simpson's trial—twelve primary jurors and twelve alternates—were sequestered for over eight months. Both the defense and prosecution wanted to make sure that the jurors could hear the case without being biased by news reports and opinion pieces that proclaimed Simpson's guilt or innocence. Due to the long time it took for evidence to be presented at Simpson's trial, ten of the original jurors had to be replaced by alternates. Finally, in early October 1995 the twelve jurors were ready to reveal Simpson's fate.

After many months of hearing the evidence, the Simpson jury deliberated for just four hours. It surprised everybody—even Simpson—when the jurors re-entered the courtroom so quickly after the trial ended. Members of the prosecution team were not even at the courthouse. As a result, the verdict was not read until the day after the jury deliberated. The jurors announced that Simpson was found "not guilty" of the murders.

Many members of the public were stunned. Had the jury not considered the large amount of evidence that seemed to indicate Simpson's guilt? Afterward, some the jurors explained some of the reasons for their decision. One claimed the prosecution had not proven that there was a long history of domestic abuse between Simpson and Brown, a key element of their case. Another asserted that a blood-covered glove found at the crime scene and presented by the prosecution as evidence did not fit Simpson, so it could not have been his. Simpson's defense attorney Johnny Cochran had commented to the jury, "If it doesn't fit, you must acquit."[1]

Some jurors admitted that although they believed Simpson had probably been involved in the murders, the

To see the reading of O.J. Simpson's verdict, scan here.

prosecution simply had not presented enough evidence to prove their case beyond a reasonable doubt. Some African American members of the jury also believed Los Angeles Police Department (LAPD) officers might have planted evidence, including the bloody glove, to implicate Simpson. The black community had long viewed the LAPD as racially biased, due to incidents like the Rodney King beating a few years earlier.

Immediately, the O.J. Simpson verdict divided people across the nation. Simpson's supporters were convinced that justice had been served. Others believed just as strongly that the justice system had failed.
The criminal justice system in the United States is highly complex, and includes both the activities of law enforcement officers as well as court proceedings. Often, social and economic factors come into play in the arrests, trials, and rehabilitation of individuals in the criminal justice system.

In O. J. Simpson's case, many people believed racism played a crucial role in his arrest. Even individuals who believed in Simpson's guilt were critical of the way the Los Angeles Police Department had investigated the crime scene and gathered evidence from Simpson's home. For example, a sock officers found in Simpson's bedroom was stained with Brown's blood—but not until after they brought it to the police lab. Staining had seeped through the sock, making it clear that Simpson could not have been wearing the sock when the blood appeared.

"It is more important that innocence be protected than it is that guilt be punished, for guilt and crimes are so frequent in this world that they cannot all be punished."[2]
  —President John Adams"

Today, many Americans recognize that there are problems with the criminal justice system. Americans are divided over the efficacy of the system and whether bias based on race, sexuality, gender, and/or socio-economic status exists in the courtroom and in law enforcement. Deep debate over issues like the death penalty, criminal justice reform, and discrimination are ongoing. To approach ideas like these, all the complexities involved must be considered.

INSTITUTIONS OF THE CRIMINAL JUSTICE SYSTEM

In the United States, the criminal justice system includes all the institutions that identify individuals who break laws and determine which punishment, **rehabilitation**, or support the government will provide.

Three specific institutions make up the criminal justice system: law enforcement, courts, and corrections. Each branch serves an essential function by establishing and enforcing the country's laws. When you consider the breakdown of the criminal justice system into city, county, state, and federal jurisdictions, you understand how complex the system can become. Without an entity encompassing the country's entire criminal justice system, some variance occurs in laws and management from state to state and from municipality to municipality.

Law enforcement officials uphold the laws of their assigned **jurisdictions**. They investigate and prevent crimes, apprehend suspects, and detain individuals accused of committing crimes. Law enforcement officers typically represent the first contact an individual has with the criminal justice system, and police officers are among the most common law enforcement personnel people encounter. Many more people work behind the scenes in law enforcement, including probation officers, prison guards, and administrators.

The courts resolve legal disputes, including criminal trials, on local, state, and federal levels. Courts also determine sentencing for criminal convictions after finding a

Police officers are responsible for maintaining public safety.

defendant guilty. Criminal trials may last days, weeks, or months. The goal of a trial is to serve justice without considering personal bias. Americans often consider the courts the branch that administers justice. The professionals who work in this branch include judges, attorneys, and **prosecutors**. A jury is also a component of this branch. Any citizen of the United States may be called on to participate as a juror in a criminal trial.

Corrections is the branch of criminal justice that administers punishment and rehabilitation. The corrections branch includes prisons, jails, and probation programs. Detention centers may house individuals awaiting trial or those convicted of criminal charges. Sentencing convicted criminals to spend time in prison (incarceration) serves several purposes. Incarceration removes a convicted criminal from society, preventing them from committing additional crimes. Additionally, prison sentences can provide an opportunity for society to rehabilitate inmates, often in the form of education and job training.

WHEN SOMEONE IS ARRESTED

In cases where a minor crime has been committed—for example, a driving violation such as speeding or not

Some studies indicate that strict punishments, including imprisonment, are helpful in deterring crime.

wearing a seatbelt—the officer will give the offender a citation, but not arrest them. The citation requires the person to appear in court for a hearing called an arraignment, in which they must plead "guilty" or "not guilty" to the charge. A magistrate will impose a fine or sentence on those who plead guilty, and will refer those who plead "not guilty" for a trial.

In more serious cases, however, police will arrest the suspect. They will question the suspect, and will search for other evidence that indicates the person committed the crime. If the police can find enough evidence, a prosecutor who works with the police department will file criminal charges, requiring the accused person to face trial.

When Americans are arrested, they are promised certain protections under the US Constitution. Among the most important rights of the accused include those afforded by the Fourth Amendment, which prohibits police from searching for illegal items or evidence of crimes without a warrant or reasonable suspicion. According to the U.S. Constitution, "the right of the people to be secure in their persons, houses, papers, and effects, against unreasonable searches and seizures, shall not be violated."[3]

The Fifth Amendment to the Constitution gives those accused of crimes the right to refuse to answer questions or make statements that might incriminate them in wrongdoing. The Sixth Amendment provides other protections, including the right to legal counsel, the right to be informed of all charges against them, and the right to a speedy and fair trial.

These rights have been affirmed and supplemented by many Supreme Court decisions over the years. The landmark case *Weeks v. United States* (1914) established that evidence obtained illegally by police cannot be used in court. *Gideon v. Wainwright* (1963) ensured that the government must provide legal counsel to accused people who cannot afford a lawyer. And *Miranda v. Arizona* (1966) determined that law enforcement officers must inform an accused individual about his or her rights before that person can be questioned while under arrest.

When a person is arrested, he or she is brought to the police station and "booked." The police gather information about the suspect, including their name, birthdate, and address. The suspect's fingerprints are taken, along with several photographs of his or her face (often called "mugshots"). Police will question the suspect about the crime, and evaluate any answers given against the evidence they have found. Once this process is complete, the prosecutor will review the case and determine whether there is enough evidence to file charges. In many states, the prosecutor must file charges within twenty-four to forty-eight hours after an arrest. This ensures that people cannot be held in prison indefinitely without being formally accused of a crime.

Often, a person who has been arrested is detained in a prison until the next step in the process, the arraignment.

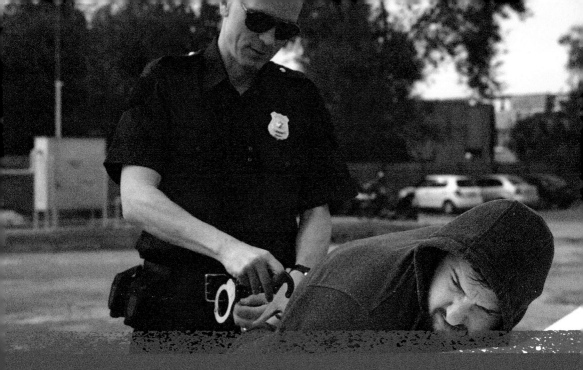

Before an arrested person is questioned by police officers, he or she must be informed that they have the right not to answer questions, and the right to have an attorney present during questioning. The statement of rights is known as the "Miranda warning," after a landmark Supreme Court case.

In most states, this arraignment must be held soon after the charges are filed. The judge reads the charges publicly against the accused person, and the accused enters a plea in response. If the accused person pleads "guilty," a hearing will follow in which the judge reviews the evidence and imposes a sentence. If the person pleads "not guilty," the judge will set a date for a trial.

In some cases, people who have pled "not guilty" to a charge may be allowed to pay a fee to the court, known as bail. This enables them to leave the prison until the trial, as long as they promise to return. The judge will determine whether bail is permitted, and in what amount. If the person appears in court for their trial, the bail payment will be returned to them. If they do not appear, the money will be forfeited and authorities will seek to arrest the person again.

WHAT HAPPENS DURING A CRIMINAL TRIAL?

In the United States, those who are accused of crimes are considered to be innocent until they are proven to be guilty. A person cannot be punished for a crime, unless he or she is convicted in a trial of committing the crime.

After the arraignment, it can take weeks or months before the trial is ready to begin. This is because both the prosecutors and the defense attorney who represents the accused person must prepare to appear in court. The prosecutors will utilize all of the evidence that police have found to present reasons why the accused person should be found guilty. The defense attorney will have access to all of the prosecutor's evidence, and will try to develop an explanation for the evidence, called a rebuttal, that shows that the accused person did not commit the crime.

When a criminal trial begins, the prosecution case is presented first. The prosecutor, who represents the government, is said to have the "burden of proof." This means the government must prove its case against the accused person "beyond a reasonable doubt." Members of a jury must be completely certain that the accused person actually committed the crime. Jurors are supposed to make their decision based only on the evidence the prosecution presents in court, as well as the defense attorney's rebuttal of that evidence.

After each party has argued its case, the jury (or judge in some cases) will decide whether the individual is guilty of the charges. An accused person who is found "not guilty" is released from prison. This person cannot face a criminal trial again for the same crime, even if new evidence comes to light later that indicates their guilt. An accused person who is convicted of a crime with a guilty verdict must return to court for sentencing. At this point, he or she enters the correctional portion of the criminal justice system.

Corrections encompasses punishments like prison and jail, but not everyone who is convicted of a crime will go to jail. Depending on the severity of the crime, some people may be placed on probation, where they are allowed to live

In nearly all criminal trials, a jury hears evidence and decides whether the accused person is innocent or guilty. Juries have no involvement in sentencing those who are found guilty; that is left to the judge who oversees the trial.

out of prison but must follow certain rules. Others may be sent to a state-sanctioned center for drug rehabilitation or mental health services. Some convicts who are sentenced to prison terms may be eligible to be released early on parole.

THE EVOLUTION OF THE CRIMINAL JUSTICE SYSTEM IN THE UNITED STATES

When the British colonies were established in North America during the sixteenth and seventeenth centuries, their criminal justice systems were based on laws and institutions that had previously been established in Europe. Over time, colonists developed their own system, which appropriated parts of England's criminal justice system. One important element was distinction of two types of crimes: misdemeanor charges, which are lesser crimes, and felony charges, which are more serious.

During colonial times, individuals accused of crimes were not guaranteed legal counsel. While some people were rich enough to afford defense attorneys, professionals usually played a small role in the overall legal process. The judge or magistrate would make a final decision of guilt or innocence.

Most people were punished at the time of sentencing, then released. Punishments for felony crimes could include whipping, public humiliation, and hanging. Misdemeanors were typically punished with fines. Imprisonment was not as common because resources were scarce. Those sen-

"Justice is not only the absence of oppression — it is the presence of opportunity. Justice is making sure that every young person knows that they are special and their lives matter. Justice is living up to the common creed that I am my brother's keeper and I am my sister's keeper. Justice and redemption go hand in hand."[4]

—President Barack Obama

tenced to jail terms were often locked in small, unsanitary rooms.

The American criminal justice system changed after the American Revolution. During the 1760s and 1770s the British had abused the system, allowing government officials to carry out searches without warrants and letting them detain people for long periods without formally charging them with crimes. These abuses angered many Americans, and were among the reasons that the Declaration of Independence was written in 1776. After the war, protections for accused criminals were written into the Bill of Rights to the US Constitution. In addition, the states began to develop their own criminal codes and punishments. In Pennsylvania, the Quakers encouraged laws that would impose punishments such as hard labor on convicted criminals, rather than execution. Over time many of the northern states outlawed physical punishments like branding and whipping. Massachusetts opened the first state prison in 1805, and other states followed suit.

Over time, two types of prisons developed in the United States. Most common was a type of prison modeled after the state prison in Auburn, New York. In the "Auburn plan" prisons, convicts would spend the day working in supervised groups, either outside the prison or in small workshops within the facility. They would return in the evening to their own cells. Although they worked with other inmates, the prisoners were not allowed to talk with each other. In Philadelphia, another type of prison developed that focused on rehabilitation. Instead of forcing the prisoners to work, they were confined in cells by themselves. Prisoners were allowed to exercise or sometimes read religious texts, but they were not allowed to communicate with other prisoners or with the guards. More than 300 prisons utilizing this "Pennsylvania system" were established around the United States during the nineteenth century.

Whipping remained a part of the criminal justice system in the southern states, as a way to control those deemed "unruly." Prisoners were also put to work outside in the fields. With the onset of the Civil War in 1861, the convicts in state prisons were often put to work producing uniforms, shoes, and other supplies for both Union and Confederate soldiers.

Following the Civil War, states began to develop systems of probation and parole as rehabilitative measures. Probation is a punishment that allows the court to release an offender with the promise that he or she will engage in good behavior. Massachusetts was the first state to implement probation on a state level, but it took longer for

Members of a chain gang in Georgia, circa 1898. In the southern states, groups of convicts were shackled together and forced to perform manual labor on public projects, such as building roads or clearing land. This form of punishment was mostly ended by the late 1950s.

federal laws to follow. The Probation Act of 1925 formally gave federal judges the authority to sentence convicted criminals to probation instead of prison terms, at their discretion. As a result of this new legislation, new organizations were set up to handle the management of probation services.

The history of parole is a bit different. The first state to enact parole sentences was New York, which established this practice in 1907. In less than forty years, every state implemented a parole system. By the 1970s, the majority of prisoners had the opportunity to achieve parole before

The Ohio State Reformatory was built between 1886 and 1910 in Mansfield, Ohio. It remained in operation until 1990.

the end of their sentence. With parole, offenders have the opportunity for supervised release so long as they demonstrate good behavior.

To combat the increasing number of parolees, the Sentencing Reform Act of 1984 placed extra requirements on individuals who are released from prison on parole from federal prisons. These requirements include educational goals and instances of good behavior. For state prisons, parole is still available on a state-by-state basis. States often use parole boards to identify which prisoners demonstrate the capacity to become part of the general public under the watchful eye of a probation officer.

THE CHANGING AMERICAN PRISON SYSTEM

Since the 1970s, the prison system has grown at an unprecedented level. As of 2018, the United States had the highest rate of incarceration in the world compared to its population. In fact, the United States is home to 22 percent of the world's prisoners while holding only 4 percent of the world's population. While incarceration rates have steadily increased, crime rates have actually decreased, which presents a puzzling narrative.

Legislation like the Anti-Drug Abuse Act of 1986 played an important role in the growing prison population. Changes in sentencing laws have also contributed to the increasing prison population. Since the 1990s, so-called "three-strikes laws" have targeted habitual offenders in many states, establishing mandatory life sentences for individuals convicted of three separate violent felonies, including sexual offenses, kidnapping, manslaughter, or armed robbery. Consequently, American prisoners tend to serve longer sentences than convicts in other countries. For example, the average prison sentence for burglary in the United States is sixteen months. In Canada, the same crime would result in a five-month sentence.

Many factors—including race, socioeconomic status, and gender—play a role in one's experience in the prison system. The degree to which each of these factors is important is a highly debated topic in America today.

Some research suggests disparity between racial groups represented in prison. For instance, about 15 percent of drug users are black Americans, but they represent 37 percent of those arrested for drug-related crimes, and 74 percent of individuals sentenced to prison for drug crimes. One of the remaining questions about the criminal justice system is how to account for such significant differences in racial composition of prison populations.

Also of note is the fact that crime rates are higher in low-income areas than in other neighborhoods. Individuals who live in low-income regions face higher likelihood of incarceration. In many of these cases, the individuals arrested are young people who may face a higher financial burden than others in the country. While some young people do benefit from programs like rehabilitation and diversion, criminal justice resources are not readily available in every region.

TEXT-DEPENDENT QUESTIONS

1. What purpose does each of three components of the criminal justice system serve?
2. What does the Fourth Amendment of the US Constitution guarantee to all Americans?
3. How have changes in mandatory sentencing laws affected the US prison population?

 RESEARCH PROJECTS

Using the Internet or your school library, research a recent criminal trial of your choosing. Identify the prosecutor, defendant, and three pieces of evidence used in the case. What was the jury's verdict? What evidence supports the idea that the defendant received a fair trial? Which amendments from the Bill of Rights were relevant to this case? Write a short essay about the case and present your findings to the class.

WORDS TO UNDERSTAND

incarceration—imprisonment.

recidivism—the re-arrest, re-conviction, or re-incarceration of an offender quickly after release.

discrimination—prejudiced treatment or action, typically negative.

CAN THE CRIMINAL JUSTICE SYSTEM BE REFORMED?

CHAPTER 2

Today, the United States houses about 4 percent of the world's population, yet it also contains less than 25 percent of the world's prison population. In fact, the United States has the highest rate of incarceration in the entire world.

Subsections of society behind bars tell researchers a lot about the current status of the criminal justice system. Since the 1970s, the rate of women imprisoned has risen 757 percent. Additionally, individuals who live in low-income areas are not only more likely to become victims of crime, but they are also more likely to be arrested and imprisoned. In spite of the fact that poverty is not a sole determining factor in incarceration rates, it clearly plays a role in increasing potential risk.

The diversity of the country's laws from state to state impacts how citizens of each specific state face imprisonment. For example, states like Arizona have an even higher incarceration rate than the national average.

Drug-related offenses are among the most common reasons for incarceration in the United States. In fact, one in five people behind bars is there for committing a drug-related crime. In the 1970s, the federal government opted

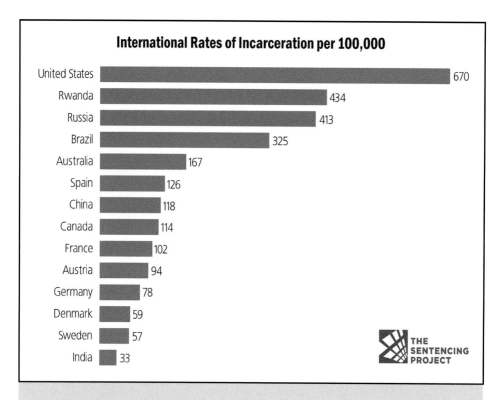

International Rates of Incarceration per 100,000

United States	670
Rwanda	434
Russia	413
Brazil	325
Australia	167
Spain	126
China	118
Canada	114
France	102
Austria	94
Germany	78
Denmark	59
Sweden	57
India	33

THE SENTENCING PROJECT

The United States is the world's leader in incarceration, with roughly 2.2 million people in the nation's prisons and jails.

to lengthen prison sentences associated with a variety of crimes. In some cases, the government created entirely new prison sentences for crimes previously resulting in small fines or jail time. Between the years 1978 and 2014, the prison population increased 408 percent. Police officers began focusing on low-level offenses, especially those linked to drug use. Offenders faced new policies when they got to court, including mandatory minimum sentencing and a lack of parole and rehabilitation opportunities.

A trend toward increased incarceration in spite of over-all declining crime rates has sparked a sense of urgency in many American citizens. Many have expressed a need for criminal justice reform, changes made to the current system to encourage a better sense of justice throughout the nation.

Criminal justice reform is attached to the concept that reducing crime and reducing the rate of incarceration go hand in hand rather than contradict each other. America's incarceration statistics are shocking, especially considering

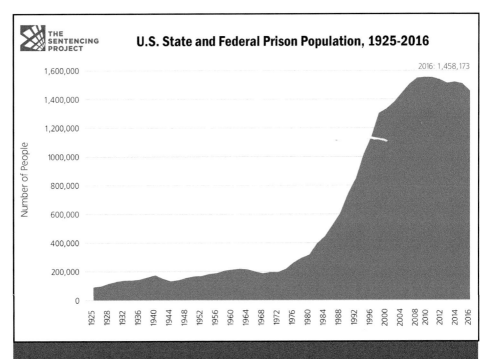

U.S. State and Federal Prison Population, 1925-2016

Much of the steady increase in the US prison population over the past forty years is a result of changes in law and policy that impose longer prison sentences, rather than increases in crime rates.

that other contenders for high incarceration rates do not come close to taking over the reins.

The following essays examine whether or not the United States has a chance of reforming its criminal justice system.

One approach to reform could be to create alternatives to imprisonment for non-violent criminal offenders.

THE CRIMINAL JUSTICE SYSTEM CAN BE REFORMED

While no single law may create a revolution in the criminal justice system, reform is possible through a series of changes to the current system. Many experts and researchers believe that implementing a variety of new laws, including those that reduce discrimination and minimize sentences for non-violent offenders, will benefit the United States by reducing crime rates and incarceration rates.

In 2014, the National Research Council found two main causes for America's increased incarceration rates. First, the council determined that longer sentences are increasing the incarceration levels at unprecedented levels. Next, the National Research Council determined that the imprisonment rates have increased in part because offenders have an increased likelihood of being caught, arrested, and convicted.

"An increase in incarceration does not always lead to a decrease in crime," said Inimai Chettiar, director of the Brennan Center's Justice Program. "This is because factors other than incarceration are what bring down crime, such as smart policing, more police, an aging population, increased income, and decreased alcohol consumption."[5]

Chettiar is not the first to discuss reducing crime rates without increasing imprisonment. In fact, other states have already done it, corroborating Chettiar's statements. In fact, the ten states with the largest decline in incarceration rates between 2008 and 2013 found ways to cut crime rates more significantly than the states facing increased incarceration rates. Thirty-one states have been able to reduce both rates between 2010 and 2015.

Perhaps one of the most effective solutions for cutting the rates of imprisonment is to examine the ways different states prosecute non-violent offenses, especially when they are linked to drug convictions. Federal prisons contain more non-violent offenders than state prisons. In fact, a large percentage of American inmates are behind bars for committing non-violent offenses. One study suggests that nearly one-quarter of all American prisoners could be deemed non-violent, and most could effectively participate in alternative methods of discipline like mental health treatment and rehabilitation.

Prison reform is not the only aspect of incarceration that reform proponents wish to focus on. Jail churn is also a high-priority concern affecting more low-income offenders than anybody else. Individuals who cannot afford cash bail are more likely to sit in jail awaiting trial. Most people in jail awaiting trial have not committed terrible crimes— they simply cannot afford to leave. The state of New Jersey addressed this issue by ending the practice of accepting cash bail. Instead, the state now requires a hearing shortly after an arrest to determine whether or not a person accused of a crime can be safely released until his or her trial. Since the state enacted this change, New Jersey's prison population has decreased significantly.

"It's a stark fact that the United States has less than five percent of the world's population, yet we have almost 25 percent of the world's total prison population. The numbers today are much higher than they were 30, 40 years ago despite the fact that crime is at historic lows."[6]

—Hillary Clinton

States can also address the strict penalties placed on youthful offenders who face drastic implications throughout the rest of their lives. More than 8,500 youths may face imprisonment for technical probation violations rather than new offenses. An additional 2,300 youths are behind bars as a result of offenses not even considered illegal by adult standards. These "crimes" include truancy and running away from home. Additionally, nearly 10 percent of these individuals are housed alongside adults.

Additionally, the criminal justice system must acknowledge systematic discrimination. For instance, some laws unfairly (albeit unintentionally) target Latino and African American communities. People of color are overrepresented in the criminal justice system. While black Americans

REFORM IN CALIFORNIA

In 2006, California governor Arnold Schwarzenegger used emergency powers to transfer more than 10,000 prison inmates to private prisons in other states. This was a reaction to prison populations increasing to an ultimate high. Later, the Republican actor-turned-politician increased rewards for county probation departments who were able to keep offenders out of state-operated prisons and also made it more difficult to send offenders back to prison if they violated parole.

Schwarzenegger struggled against federal judges and the Supreme Court to make changes to the California criminal justice system. While state legislation tried to limit the role of three-strikes legislation to prevent prison overcrowding, Schwarzenegger found fit to move prisoners instead.

After federal judges ordered California to address prison crowding, Schwarzenegger signed a bill to authorize one of the state's largest prison construction projects. The governor also had other plans for the make up about 40 percent of the population behind bars, they represent only 13 percent of those living in the United States.

The government can also address discrimination by developing better indigent defense programs for their members who may not be able to afford lawyers. The Sixth Amendment to the U.S. Constitution guarantees each defendant in criminal court the "right . . . to have the assis-

facilities. "In the critical few months before an inmate is released, our re-entry facilities will focus on job training and placement, on education, on anger management, substance abuse and family counseling, and housing placement," he said.[7] While the plan was ultimately a bipartisan project, criticism by experts and lawmakers suggested that the construction would fail to address the heart of the problems with the criminal justice system.

Other politicians criticized the project, suggesting that the state's needs call for sentencing reform rather than new prisons. Gloria Romero, Senate Democratic Majority Leader, claimed the bill "was a prop that the governor asked for so he can walk into court and look like he's tough on crime."[8]

Attempts at criminal justice reform are ongoing in California. Ongoing legislation and social service program reformation may help shed new light on the future of the state's criminal justice system.

tance of counsel for his defense."[9] State proceedings did not take on this right until the Supreme Court ruled in the case of *Gideon v. Wainwright* (1963), in which they determined an indigent person was entitled to defense counsel at the state's expense. Unfortunately, this defense is not always the most effective because the attorneys assigned to provide it are often undertrained, underfunded, and lacking in resources.

Criminal justice reform also revolves around building trust between members of law enforcement and the communities they serve. Some cities have initiated programs promoting mentoring and ambassadorship as possible solutions for developing relationships with individuals the police are not commonly in positive contact with.

Local law enforcement personnel can also strengthen community bonds by making citizens more aware of the services awaiting them. Addiction treatment centers and housing shelters could benefit a percentage of people who might otherwise be arrested for possession or cited for loitering. Law enforcement professionals should build a reputation for providing positive benefits to those they serve.

President Obama took some steps toward developing relationships between communities and the law enforcement personnel serving them. He promoted the use of body cameras to record officer and suspect movements. These cameras could provide additional insight into the actions officers and suspects took, establishing accountability and potential evidence.

Obama's administration also emphasized the need to expand community-oriented policing. This model encourages law enforcement officers to build strong bonds that facilitate reducing crime.

Finally, the criminal justice system should emphasize the role of successful re-entry of incarcerated individuals back into society. Successful re-entry into society prevents

It can be very difficult for convicts to find a job after their release from prison, and studies indicate this results in higher rates of recidivism. A successful reform program could include more programs to teach prison inmates a trade, such as carpentry or pipefitting, that could help them get a good job after they have served their sentence. Programs could also help inmates complete high school educations and develop skills that can be used in the modern workforce.

recidivism, or the likelihood of an individual being arrested and imprisoned again.

As it currently stands, released offenders have a difficult time finding gainful employment in spite of the fact that regular work is one of the first stepping stones to prevent recidivism. One study suggested that only 12.5 percent of employers would be willing to hire individuals who had been incarcerated in the past. "Ironically, getting back to work decreases recidivism, but there are barriers for ex-convicts finding work," noted the report from the Simmons University School of Social Work in Boston. "Many prisoners have limited education and work experience, which makes it difficult for them to secure employment after they are released."[10]

Is the criminal justice system broken? Find out what senators, police officers, activists, and others think here.

The Big Question

IS OUR CRIMINAL JUSTICE SYSTEM BROKEN?

Filmed by *The Atlantic* at the Aspen Ideas Festival, 2015

0:00 | 0:00

Prisons currently offer limited opportunities for educational and skill development behind bars. Studies show that about 70 percent of incarcerated individuals did not graduate from high school. Without educational opportunities, many prisoners are released with few prospects on the horizon.

Many people with felonies in their history also struggle to secure housing. They may lack a credit history to secure an apartment, or perhaps the felony prohibits them from living in certain housing complexes. The lack of housing options can actually promote recidivism.

Familial relationships also suffer for individuals in prison. Many offenders find themselves entirely dependent upon family members upon release, but in many cases, they have had limited contact over the course of their incarceration. Prisons may facilitate strong relationships among family members by offering privileges for individuals who participate in programs like parenting courses, for instance. Prisons have tried programs like these in the past, but program participation eventually declined. Facilitating the program early on in one's sentence may help keep bonds strong for a better return home.

The non-partisan desire to address criminal justice reform bodes well for the future of projects addressing incarceration and recidivism. Results of several polls suggest widespread support for reform, including decreasing the prison population, spending less money on incarceration, and increasing the safety of all American communities.

THE CRIMINAL JUSTICE SYSTEM CANNOT BE REFORMED

The criminal justice system evolves naturally over time to meet the demands of the country and its citizens. The current laws in place are meant to protect the rights of victims and to prevent Americans from being victimized by crime. The desire of many Americans to change the criminal justice system notwithstanding, many issues prevent any significant change from occurring.

Many lawmakers are willing to address issues associated with criminal justice reform, but the truth of the matter is that the individual issues involved in reform are far too partisan-based to see any dramatic change. Senators Rand Paul and Cory Booker, a Republican and Democrat respectively, have jointly proposed programs to ease sentences on juvenile offenders. The truth is that many senators are not willing to extend an olive branch across the aisle to address issues together. The future of criminal justice reform remains uncertain because legislators often fail to come up with actionable goals to achieve it.

Changing the criminal justice system requires understanding the issues and partisanship that have prevented legislation from being passed. Even changing presidents affects the direction of the criminal justice system. For instance, during his term (2009–2017) President Barack Obama, a Democrat, emphasized the need to reduce long prison sentences for non-violent offenders, particularly those with minor drug offenses. When Donald Trump, a

Unfortunately, over the past two decades a growing spirit of partisanship has made it nearly impossible for Republicans and Democrats in Congress to work together on programs that would benefit all Americans, such as reform of the criminal justice system.

Republican, took office as president in 2017, his attorney general instructed federal prosecutors to seek harsher punishments for individuals with drug offenses.

Prison reform is not going to be free, and American taxpayers disagree over the best way to reduce costs while providing appropriate justice. Some taxpayers want to reduce the amount of time prisoners spend on death row as a cost-cutting option, while others strictly oppose the death penalty and prefer that criminals be imprisoned for life, a more expensive proposition. Some taxpayers want convicts to have educational opportunities while in prison, as studies show this can prevent recidivism; others oppose state and federal funds going toward any form of self-improvement or educational programs for prison inmates. Preventing individuals from entering the criminal justice system altogether will also be expensive, considering the cost of state-funded rehabilitation programs and social services for those living in poverty.

Next, intense disagreement exists as to how militarized police forces should be. One of the most contentious issues among those invested in criminal justice reform is whether or not communities can trust militarized law enforcement personnel. With federal programs providing local police forces with military-type weaponry and tactics, legislators on both sides are unsure how to proceed.

When news media reports stories about police brutality, it brings negative attention to all law enforcement personnel. When police officers feel threatened by hostile and

Operations by federal agencies like the Drug Enforcement Agency (DEA) and Immigrations and Customs Enforcement (ICE) are necessary to stop narcotics trafficking and reduce the spread of drugs and crime.

distrusting constituents, militarization may be the only way to provide adequate protection. More police officers could die without the protection offered by lethal weapons.

Additionally, studies indicate that police departments with greater resources are more likely to catch criminals. One of the best deterrents for crime is the perception by a potential offender that he or she will be caught. A strong police force may provide a greater deterrent than an unmilitarized force.

In addressing issues of police militarization and force, criminal justice reform proponents may find a stronger argument in addressing the lack of formal training with military-type equipment. This may leave officers and departments lacking the essential skills to using the items in the situations where they might be the most necessary.

Finally, proponents of criminal justice reform often decry prison time for non-violent offenses and drug-related convictions. The truth is that strict punishments, including imprisonment, are often necessary to deter crime. Prisons can provide a necessary tool to prevent offenders from creating larger problems. After all, a burglar who is in prison will not break into more homes. A drug dealer behind bars is not selling illegal substances to children.

One study in the United Kingdom suggests that longer prison sentences and higher levels of police activity are more likely to decrease criminal activity, especially when discussing property crimes committed by repeat and serious offenders. The study suggests that increasing burglary sentences by just one month could significantly reduce the number of burglaries committed in one year. The study also suggests that when sentences are reduced, so that offenders only serve a portion of their initial prison time, it can lead to increased crime.

Criminal justice reform proponents should consider that perhaps the problem is not the type of punishment in America but rather the epidemic of violence throughout the country. While reform may address the prison population, this may be treating a symptom rather than curing the problem. Reducing prison sentences will not resolve the problems of mental illness, racial discrimination, or poverty.

Statistics suggest that 20 percent of incarcerated individuals are behind bars due to drug offenses. While those opposed to prison sentences for drug offenders have a history of violence, the bigger point is that most are not sent to prison for possessing a tiny amount of an illegal substance. Often, those serving long sentences have a long history of criminal behavior. The percentage of individuals in prison based on drug offenses are not necessarily non-violent. Drug trafficking has fatal consequences, and many offenders are involved with high-level trading.

Criminal justice reform is not likely in the near future based not only on partisan-level legislation, but also because practical alternatives are not readily available. If more resources were available to create a solid plan for reform, a chance might emerge for a new type of justice.

TEXT-DEPENDENT QUESTIONS

1. What steps did Arnold Schwarzenegger take in California to influence criminal justice reform? How did people respond to these steps?

2. What did the National Research Council pinpoint as the cause of increased incarceration?

3. What are two possible deterrents for crime in the United States?

 # RESEARCH PROJECTS

Take a look at the State-by-State Data for incarceration from the Sentencing Project (available at https://www.sentencingproject.org/the-facts/#map). What is the incarceration rate for your state? How has the rate changed over time? What do you think prompted these changes? Do you see any discrepancies in race, age, or income level? What steps has your state taken to impact criminal justice reform? Write a two-page paper discussing your findings and assessing whether or not criminal justice reform has been effective.

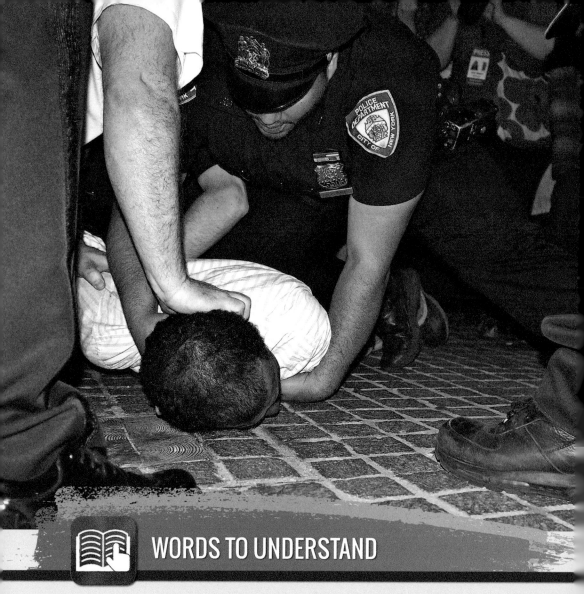

de facto—existing in fact, even without legal authority

exonerate—to be found innocent of a crime, or not responsible for wrongdoing.

minorities—a relatively small group of people who are often treated differently from the rest of the population due to racial, religious, linguistic, or other characteristics.

racial profiling—the use of characteristics such as race or ethnicity to identify those believed more likely to have committed a crime.

DOES RACIAL DISCRIMINATION PLAY A ROLE IN THE CRIMINAL JUSTICE SYSTEM?

CHAPTER 3

On September 16, 2016, Terence Crutcher, a forty-year-old black man, was shot and killed by a white Tulsa police officer, Betty Jo Shelby. Crutcher's shooting is one of many that have been widely publicized in the past decade because it involved the death of a black person at the hands of white police officers.

Many people feel racial discrimination is a leading factor in the decision by police to use lethal force. Crutcher had been standing in the street near his vehicle when he was shot, and he had no weapon on his person or in his vehicle. As a result, his family, friends, and groups like the American Civil Liberties Union and Black Lives Matter called for Shelby to be charged with his murder. Shelby was charged by the state with "unlawfully and unnecessarily" killing Crutcher, but after a homicide investigation she was acquitted of first-degree manslaughter charges on May 17, 2017.

Defenders of the police officer noted that Crutcher had abandoned his vehicle in the middle of the street before police arrived, and had been acting erratically. Videos of the confrontation showed that Crutcher did not obey when police officers told him to stop or to lie down in the street.

Instead, Crutcher walked back to his vehicle and seemed to be trying to reach inside. The officers believed he posed a threat. Shelby's partner, Tyler Turnbough, shot Crutcher with a Taser electroshock weapon at the same time that Shelby fired her service weapon. An autopsy found that Crutcher had been using powerful hallucinogenic drugs shortly before the incident. These facts undoubtedly contributed to the finding that Shelby was not guilty of manslaughter. However, for many people, a key question remained: would such an encounter have resulted in a shooting if the suspect had been white?

In recent years, racial discrimination in the criminal justice system has become a major issue. Individuals who believe racial discrimination plays a significant role in today's criminal justice system cite statistics demonstrating that a disproportionate number of black and Latino Americans are incarcerated, though those on the other side of the issue may claim that other factors, like poverty and educational levels, are bigger factors involved in the system than race.

Laws against discrimination are meant to protect individuals of all races from becoming targets of the system. Discrimination on the basis of race is illegal, but individuals who claim discrimination exists in the current criminal justice system may suggest it happens more covertly and often even without consciousness.

The essays that follow will examine two sides of the issue of racial discrimination.

RACIAL DISCRIMINATION SIGNIFICANTLY IMPACTS THE CRIMINAL JUSTICE SYSTEM

Individuals who believe racial discrimination plays a significant role in the criminal justice system have many reasons for believing this to be true. Many contend that statistics tell the entire story, whereas others may point to specific laws designed to place certain types of individuals behind bars more often than others.

According to the Bureau of Justice Statistics, 32 percent of black men and 17 percent of Latino men born in 2001 should expect to spend time in prison. As disheartening as this statistic is, it does not surprise many people who have

"Black lives are too easy to take in America because we don't want to question why people are so afraid of black and brown people to begin with."[10]
—African-American filmmaker Yance Ford, whose brother's murder was the subject of his documentary Strong Island

been watching the trends. The incarceration rates of racial **minorities** are significantly higher than the incarceration rate for white Americans.

Racial minorities are also much more likely to become victims of crime. "The communities most harmed by crime and violence are the least supported by the criminal justice system," said Aswad Thomas, a victim's services coordinator for the Alliance for Safety and Justice. "What these commu-

The "Black Lives Matter" movement was formed to protest numerous cases in which black Americans were killed during encounters with police.

Scan here to learn more about the role racial discrimination may play in the court system.

nities need is more investment in prevention, more investment in treatment, and more investment in community organizations that serve victims within the community."[12]

Consider the fact that black Americans are more likely to serve time for drug charges even when you consider that they use drugs at approximately the same rate as white Americans. In examining Kentucky's population, researchers discovered that black Americans make up about 8 percent of the state's residents but also 36 percent of all arrests for marijuana possession. This means that people who are black are more than three times as likely to be arrested for marijuana possession. Why aren't white people just as likely to be arrested for possession in spite of their equal use?

When cases involving drugs finally make it to court, racial minorities are much more likely than white Americans to be convicted of the crimes they are charged with. Additionally, black Americans are more likely to face harsher sentences related to drug crimes.

Part of the reason for the high discrepancy in incarceration rates is linked to a poverty disparity. Black and Latino Americans are more likely to rely on court-appointed criminal defenders rather than hiring criminal defense attorneys. The fact that so many public defenders are overworked and underfunded leaves much to be desired in terms of defense opportunities. Many people never even meet their defense attorneys until it is time to come for court.

Inadequate legal defense comes with a higher chance of false conviction. Eric Holder, a former US attorney general, claimed to witness instance of this himself. According to the Innocence Project, more than 360 people have been **exonerated** due to DNA evidence after originally being convicted of crimes they did not commit despite the efforts of overburdened public defenders. One such case was that of Eddie Joe Lloyd, a black man who spent 17 years in prison for rape and murder only to be exonerated by DNA evidence in 2002. The public defender who represented Lloyd did not investigate the case, nor did he talk to police about a false confession Lloyd made. The state of Michigan ended up footing a bill close to five million dollars in appeals, imprisonment, and a wrongful conviction settlement.

When researchers examine the statistics, they see the racial divide in exonerations demonstrating possible discriminatory practices in the criminal justice system. African Americans like Eddie Joe Lloyd make up 61 percent of the more than 360 DNA exonerations within the United States, notes the Innocence Project. According to the National Registry of Exonerations, a collaborative project involving the University of California Irvine, the University of Michigan Law School, and Michigan State University College of Law, there have been over 2,265

Blacks and Latinos who live in poor communities are more likely to be arrested for drug-related crimes than white Americans.

exonerations since 1989. A March 2017 study, "Race and Wrongful Conviction in the United States," found that 47 percent of those exonerated were black—a far greater figure than the 13 percent share of African Americans in the US population. "Most innocent defendants who have been exonerated in the United States in the past 28 years are African Americans—almost half of the nearly 2,000 individual exonerations that we know about, and the great majority of a similar number of group exonerations," noted the study's authors. "There is every reason to believe that this is also true of the much larger group of all wrongful

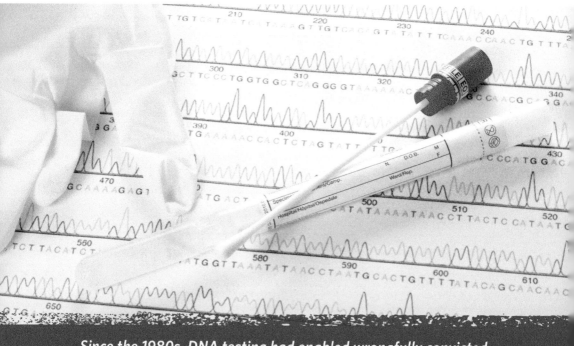

Since the 1980s, DNA testing had enabled wrongfully convicted people to be freed from prison. A high number of those exonerated are African Americans, indicating that blacks are more likely to be falsely accused and convicted than whites are.

criminal convictions."[13] The study conclusions included the statements, "Black suspects and defendants are more likely to be the targets of police and prosecutorial misconduct," and "Many innocent black defendants encounter bias and discrimination throughout their ordeals."[14]

The unfortunate truth about exonerations is that most wrongful convictions go undiscovered. Many people will stay behind bars for the rest of their lives due to unethical and illegal practices by white professionals in the criminal justice system.

Racial discrimination has also been a factor for individuals in the jury booth. In fact, cases involving the racial makeup of jurors have gone to the Supreme Court for assessment. While in the past race was used to keep racial minorities off of juries, a Supreme Court ruling in *Foster v. Chatman* (2016) made the practice more difficult. In this case, prosecutors were accused of overtly trying to prevent black citizens from being part of a jury. They went as far as to write about the plan in their notes, creating a ranking system for the black members of the jury pool.

Now, this is not to say that every instance of racism is conscious and overt. In many cases, discrimination is the culmination of insensitivity and of subtle, subconscious fear. Everybody, from judges to parole board members, may participate in **de facto** discrimination. Claiming that racial discrimination plays a role in our current system does not mean that anybody is trying to be racist. It means that laws are not in place to prevent racist practice.

RACIAL DISCRIMINATION DOES NOT SIGNIFICANTLY IMPACT THE CRIMINAL JUSTICE SYSTEM

Although some people claim that racial discrimination plays a role in the way the criminal justice system plays out today, they are overlooking many other factors. While individual officers, judges, and prosecutors certainly have their own privileges and discriminatory ways of thinking, it may be a reach to say that the entire criminal justice system is racist.

Many individuals examining racism in the criminal justice system overlook the role poverty plays. The median income of incarcerated individuals is approximately 41 percent lower than the income of those who do not go to prison.

Many individuals who discuss racism in the criminal justice system neglect to discuss the role of age. Studies suggest that older offenders receive more lenient treatment than younger offenders. Older offenders are less likely to receive a prison sentence, and when they are sentenced to prison they are less likely to be handed long sentences. Older men were more likely than older women to receive shorter sentences, bringing up questions of sexism as well. The only time when this age advantage does not seem to matter much is when it comes to defendants facing drug charges.

Additionally, individuals looking for examples of discrimination should consider the role education plays in a person's likelihood to be incarcerated. Education levels are

A person's educational status and socioeconomic level may affect the length of sentences as much or more than their racial background.

linked to increasing rates of poverty in racial minorities, and it can also indicate which white Americans are more likely to be incarcerated. Individuals who never become literate face an increased likelihood of incarceration, no matter their race. In fact, some states use their own literacy rankings to determine how much space they need to create in their prisons in the coming years.

Rather than consider the role of racism in the criminal justice system, it may be wise to examine the effects of racial issues across the board. For instance, black Americans are less likely to finish high school than white Americans. Improving the educational system for minority students might be more useful than trying to address individu-

People who are addicted to drugs or alcohol would benefit more from rehabilitation programs then from prison, but such programs are often not available—especially to those at the lower socioeconomic levels.

al prejudices in the criminal justice system. Increases in crime are also linked to declines in job opportunities. When unskilled workers are considered less necessary than those in other roles, crime may become a more alluring way to make ends meet. Additionally, many former inmates struggle to find work after they have been released from prison, leading to potentially higher rates of recidivism.

Criticism of the criminal justice system should also include a closer look at mental illness and addiction, both of which play critical roles in the criminal justice system. Individuals with addictions may benefit from social and community programs, but funds are often not available to assist people with these problems.

While individuals who promote racial discrimination as the main cause of inequality in the criminal justice system will discuss the problem of longer sentences for African-American inmates, they should also consider the fact that defendants with prior convictions are also more likely to receive longer sentences, even for non-violent offenses. States with three-strikes legislation might even allow a minor offense to result in a prison term if the defendant already has two convictions. The same rules apply in cases involving mandatory minimum sentences. The judge has no racial bias in determining the sentence if that decision has already been made via legislation.

The courts also examine aggravating factors that might lead to harsher sentences during criminal trials. Aggravating factors might include the use of a weapon or the victim's level of injury. This is to say that the courts do not examine an individual's race and make a decision based on this information alone. The judge assesses a variety of factors before sentencing an individual to prison.

Another major issue people point out when discussing discrimination in the criminal justice system is **racial profiling**. While the police force does use profiling, race is typically not the sole factor in assessing whether or not somebody is a suspect. Suspects are determined based on

"You have young men of color in many communities who are more likely to end up in jail or in the criminal justice system than they are in a good job or in college."[15]

—Barack Obama

many factors, including clothing style, age, hairstyle, possessions, and height.

Recently, racial issues have been brought to the forefront as a result of police shootings. While not every shooting may be justified in the eyes of the law, many of these cases involve officers who are following their training to preserve their own lives. Police recruits often view a video of the 1998 murder of a Georgia deputy sheriff named Kyle Dinkheller. He pulled over a man in what seemed to be a routine traffic stop. However, the driver, Andrew Brannan, did not obey Dinkheller's repeated commands. Dinkheller's hesitance to shoot enabled Brannan to grab a high-powered rifle, which he used to kill the deputy.

Dinkheller was just twenty-two years old, and he had a pregnant wife and child at home when he was killed. All police officers want to return home to their families after their shift, and so police officer training over the past twenty years has encouraged the use of force when a

Police do use profiling to identify potential wrongdoers, but race is often just one factor that is considered.

suspect does not cooperate with the police or displays an aggression.

In order to assess the possibility of discrimination in the criminal justice system, researchers must also examine the percentage of arrestees who are black, which is about 28.9 percent. The percentage of police shootings involving black victims is just slightly higher than this figure, at 31.8 percent. Keep in mind that African Americans are more likely to have contact with police officers on a regular basis, and many of these encounters are free of racial bias.

Some analysts suggest that even if we were to remove the individual racial biases that some police officers have, it would not affect the rate at which black Americans are killed by police officers. These individual officers may not be to blame for the current circumstances in the criminal justice system. Police officers must often work with a lack of clarity and specific detail about the criminals they are looking for. They also often work in poor neighborhoods stricken by high crime, because this is where they are most needed.

Rather than seeing racial discrimination as the major factor involved in tainting the criminal justice system, it may be more effective to focus on other issues at play considering societal structure and policy. We should consider a more holistic approach to the matter rather than assessing only one potential facet.

TEXT-DEPENDENT QUESTIONS

1. What is a consequence of inadequate legal defense?
2. How are racial minorities affected by educational and financial disparities?
3. Which racial group is more likely to spend time in prison for a drug offense?

 RESEARCH PROJECTS

Explore the National Registry of Exonerations, available at http://www.law.umich.edu/special/exoneration/Pages/detaillist.aspx. Select one case that stands out to you and read more about the specific case. Then, see if you can find at least one more source, like a news article, about this case. Write a report summarizing this specific case and what information led to exoneration. Did race, poverty, or education play a role in this individual's conviction.

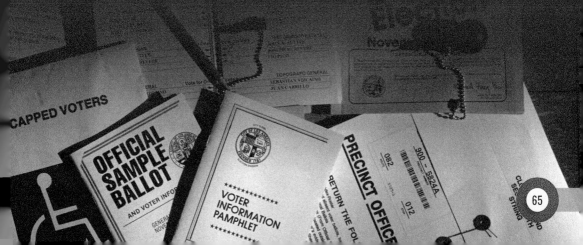

WORDS TO UNDERSTAND

abolish—to end something.

draconian—excessive, harsh, or severe

drug trafficking—involvement in the illegal cultivation, manufacture, distribution, and sale of illegal drugs.

mandatory minimum sentence—a punishment, established by law, in which an individual must be imprisoned for a predetermined period after being convicted of a crime. Judges have no leeway to take mitigating factors into account.

SHOULD MANDATORY MINIMUM SENTENCES BE ABOLISHED?

CHAPTER 4

Mandatory minimum sentences require judges to pass down sentences for certain crimes based on criteria that has been established by federal law. The judge is required to issue the sentence even when extenuating circumstances may apply. The sentencing rules are, effectively, set in stone.

Legislators lengthened certain penalties in response to increased crime during the 1970s and 1980s. In the mid-1980s, Congress passed the Comprehensive Crime Control Act. This program established some mandatory minimum sentences at the federal level. It also eliminated parole for certain inmates in federal prisons.

One of the main examples of mandatory minimum sentencing comes from the Anti-Drug Abuse Act of 1986. This act required a minimum sentence of five years imprisonment based on drug convictions involving specific amounts of substances. In the case of crack cocaine, the five-year prison sentence applied to those found with five grams of the drug. In the case of powder cocaine, the sentence applied to those with 500 grams of the substance.

Why the difference? By the mid-1980s, crack cocaine had become a very popular drug because it was inexpensive and powerful. Many of those who used it lived in poor neighborhoods, and crime rates soared in these areas as people sought money for drugs. Lawmakers believed that taking crack users off the streets would reduce crime. The law also targeted drug dealers, as someone caught with 500 grams of powder cocaine was probably planning to sell it in smaller quantities. But what this meant was that convicted crack users—most of whom were poor African Americans living in urban neighborhoods—were treated the same as hard-core drug dealers, while recreational cocaine users—who were more likely to be young white professionals—received much lighter sentences.

In some iterations, mandatory minimum sentencing legislation is marketed as "truth in sentencing laws." Alongside mandatory minimums or three-strikes legislation, this means that individuals who are sentenced to a specific amount of time will not face early release, even for

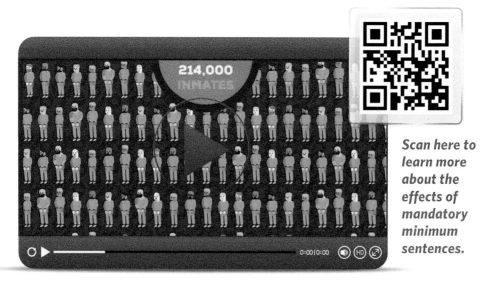

Scan here to learn more about the effects of mandatory minimum sentences.

"The policy of mandatory minimum sentencing has led to thousands of people serving longer jail sentences and has contributed to the unfair sentencing disparities between federal crack and powder cocaine offenses that disproportionately affect people of color."[16]
—Marc Mauer, Executive Director of the Sentencing Project

parole. These sentencing laws are often used in conjunction with each other.

Individuals who support mandatory minimums claim that the sentencing guidelines protect American communities by keeping criminals behind bars, while those who oppose mandatory minimums suggest it minimizes the role of judges while continuing to support discrimination in the criminal justice system. Many activists are leading the call to **abolish** mandatory minimum sentences, while others are focused on increasing these minimums.

The essays that follow will examine two sides of mandatory minimum sentencing in the United States.

MANDATORY MINIMUM SENTENCES SHOULD BE ABOLISHED

Mandatory minimum sentencing is a controversial topic in the world of criminal justice. For many reasons, mandatory minimum sentences are **draconian** and impractical. Judges should have the power to ensure that the punishment fits the crime.

One of the biggest problems associated with mandatory minimum sentencing laws is that they do not allow the judge to consider special circumstances. This means that individuals may receive harsh penalties not necessarily appropriate for the crime they were convicted of committing. For instance, an individual may spend five years in prison the first time they ever possess a drug—even if they are not involved in trafficking or selling. For instance, individuals who mailed packages without knowing the contents were

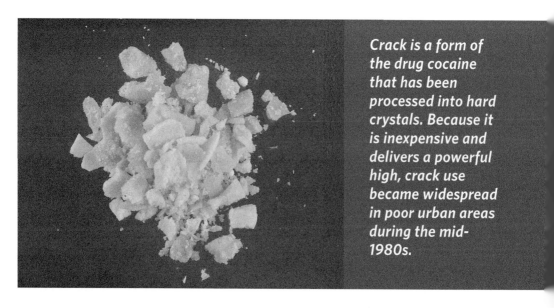

Crack is a form of the drug cocaine that has been processed into hard crystals. Because it is inexpensive and delivers a powerful high, crack use became widespread in poor urban areas during the mid-1980s.

The Anti-Drug Abuse Act of 1986 established a mandatory five-year prison sentence for possession of 100 grams (about 3.5 ounces) of powder cocaine. The same mandatory sentence applied for crack cocaine at a much smaller amount. A person caught with one gram of crack would get a five-year prison sentence.

illegal drugs could be sentenced to prison for the same amount of time as active **drug traffickers**.

Ultimately, mandatory minimum sentencing takes power away from the judge and hands it to the prosecutors. Judges are entrusted with an important role in our criminal justice system based on their years of accumulating wisdom regarding the law. In states lacking mandatory minimum sentences, judges are able to consider a variety of factors to determine the appropriate sentence for each case. For example, judges typically consider the defendant's criminal history, specific role in the crime, mental state, and severity of any injuries resulting from the incident. When society imposes mandatory minimum sentences, it does not allow judges to identify real issues and threats.

When prosecutors possess more power than judges, they may press charges based on their own agendas. They know that if the defendant is found guilty, he or she will face a specific type of punishment rather than any potential sentence the judge might hand down. This might provide an incentive for prosecutors to charge defendants with the crimes that might land the strictest possible punishment. They might also target people with certain racial or socioeconomic characteristics that they perceive to participate in criminal behavior more often than others. Additionally, prosecutors may decide whether or not to charge an individual with a harsher crime based on their gender, race, or criminal background.

Additionally, a jury could actually be influenced by the mere fact of knowing that the defendant, if convicted, faces a mandatory minimum sentence that jury members deem is too harsh. When used in conjunction with three-strikes legislation, this is especially true. The punishment for a minor third infraction may be considered cruel and inhumane for that specific offense. The jury may not be willing to send an individual to prison for the rest of their life because of a drug possession charge.

Mandatory minimum sentencing laws may also unfairly target certain demographics in spite of the fact that they are meant to take prejudice out of the picture entirely. The discrimination is built into the law. For example, black

Americans are more likely to be charged with drug offenses than white Americans, so they are more likely to face mandatory minimum sentences. Additionally, the punishment is harsher for drugs commonly associated with racial minorities and poverty, such as crack cocaine. Additionally, the communities with minimum sentencing in place could make more stringent laws to focus on these crimes rather than on other offenses.

There is also a financial reason to do away with mandatory minimum sentences: They lead to overcrowding of prisons, which is expensive. In fact, this country spends about $181 billion on incarceration each year, achieving a similar level of public safety as in 1975 for the cost of just $7.4 billion.

Some studies show that incarceration is not necessarily effective for reducing some types of crimes, especially those committed by youth or by larger groups. Studies

Mandatory minimum sentences take power away from judges, who are supposed to be impartial, and turns it over to prosecutors.

also suggest that incarceration does not deter drug crime. In fact, some studies suggest that increased incarceration might actually increase crime. Not only do prisons fail to set up their inmates for the future, but they may also act as places of education to learn to commit crime more stealthily in the future. Since the year 2000, increased prisons and jails may have contributed absolutely nothing to the reduced crime rates in this country. Instead, decreased

THE CASE OF LEANDRO ANDRADE

In November of 1995, a California man named Leandro Andrade stole several VHS tapes from two different K-Mart stores in a two-week period. He was 37 years old, a veteran of the army, and a man facing drug addiction. The value of his haul was $153.

By the time he was arrested for stealing the VHS tapes, Andrade had a history with the California and federal criminal justice systems. His previous convictions included petty theft, residential burglary, escaping from prison, and transporting marijuana. California had recently passed "three-strikes legislation," under which an individuals' third felony conviction would result in a mandatory sentence of twenty-five years to life in prison. Typically, the petty theft Andrade committed would be considered crime rates are largely attributed to aging, increased wages, increased education, and changes in policing strategies.

Individuals who are released from prison are more likely to return to crime after a long sentence imposed by mandatory minimum sentences as a result of social and cultural stigma. Individuals leaving prison have reduced employment opportunities and a lower earning potential. Increased incarceration may also promote additional crime by removing adults from their families, depriving their children of parents who may be able to provide emotional and financial support.

a misdemeanor. Instead of pursuing this charge, prosecutors opted to charge him with two counts of "petty theft with a prior," a felony.

Facing a lengthy prison for the theft of nine VHS tapes, Andrade and his lawyer sought to have his petty theft charges reduced to misdemeanors. The court declined, and Andrade was convicted and sentenced to fifty years in prison—twenty-five year for each charge. Andrade fought his conviction, arguing that the sentence violated the Eighth Amendment's prohibition on "cruel and unusual punishment." No appeals court overturned the sentence, and when the case was reviewed by the Supreme Court in 2003, it ruled 5-4 that the sentence was not cruel and unusual.

Mandatory minimum sentencing could perhaps be used as a means of coercion. For example, individuals who are facing five years in prison due to mandatory minimums for marijuana possession might seek a plea bargain instead. They may give false information to investigators in the hopes that it will help them secure a bargain and avoid the five-year sentence they know is coming.

One potential way to reduce crime associated with drugs while also saving money might be to consider the use of drug courts. Drug courts focus on sentencing individuals with addiction to treatment programs, rather than sending them to prison. The hope is that successful completion of the treatment program will reduce future drug use. Could this be a more cost-effective method than mandatory minimum sentencing?

Finally, consider that the sentences associated with mandatory minimums do little to treat any underlying issues linked to criminal behavior. For instance, mandatory minimum sentencing does not provide treatment or rehabilitation for individuals charged with drug possession, which they might actually benefit from. Could housing these individuals in prison be more expensive than providing treatment options?

In the same vein, mandatory minimum sentences do not necessarily deter people from buying, using, and selling drugs. The evidence supporting mandatory minimums for drug offenses is not strong enough to suggest it significantly impacts the availability of these substances. Local and state governments might have more power to influence drug use in their regions based on the area's needs.

While critics of eliminating mandatory minimum sentencing claim these programs would not be cost-effective, the studies have shown that offenders are not necessarily deterred by the amount of time they may spend behind bars. They are more deterred by the level of certainty they

Prisoners at the Dade County Correctional Facility in Florida.

have about being arrested and convicted. When judges sentence these individuals to prison, excessive time they spend behind bars does not necessarily return any value.

Examine the case of South Carolina, a state that reformed sentencing practices in 2010. In eight years, South Carolina was able to close down two prisons and save millions of dollars. Additionally, the state experienced a decrease in crime. The neighboring state of Georgia experienced a similar decline in crime after reforming its own sentencing practices.

In the end, the criminal justice system is meant to provide a sense of completeness, righting a wrong. Mandatory minimum sentences simply do not do this, especially because it is difficult to determine if decreases in crime are actually linked to the practice or if they are instead related to other factors, like increased education or a better economy.

MANDATORY MINIMUM SENTENCES SHOULD NOT BE ABOLISHED

Mandatory minimum sentencing serves a crucial role in our criminal justice system by establishing ground rules. Individuals who commit specific types of crimes are guaranteed to spend time in prison, no matter who the judge is. This sets a precedent and deterrent for how the courts treat criminal behavior.

To begin, take a look at the impact of mandatory minimum sentencing on crime reduction. Overall, crime has decreased throughout the country since the 1980s, when mandatory minimum sentences began to become more common. Individuals who do not want to go to prison for long stretches of time may think twice about committing crimes.

Mandatory minimum sentencing eliminates the threat of personal bias or sympathy by judges in the criminal justice system. Judges may have their own opinions about specific crimes and types of defendants. Mandatory minimums prevent judges from administering justice in a discriminatory manner. Equality exists for all people convicted of the same crime.

Take into account the case of Brock Turner, a white college student convicted of sexually assaulting a woman at Stanford University in 2015. The judge in his case, Aaron Persky, sentenced Turner to six months in jail, followed by three years of probation. Persky cited the circumstances of the case for his lenient sentence, and Turner was out of

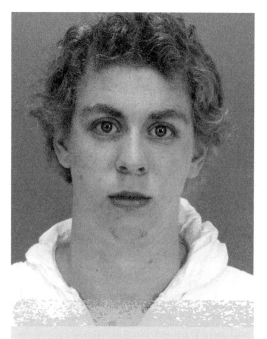

Many Americans were outraged when Brock Turner received a light sentence after being caught sexually assaulting an unconscious young woman on the college campus. A mandatory minimum sentence would have ensured a more appropriate punishment.

prison after three months. Had there been mandatory minimum sentencing in place, Turner would have served a sentence more appropriate for the crime of sexual assault. In fact, the California legislature soon passed a law requiring at least a three-year prison term for rape convictions.

Another truth about mandatory minimum sentencing is that it protects society for a longer period of time. When criminals are behind bars, they are not free to participate in other types of criminal activities that damage society. This is particularly linked to property crime. The longer an individual is behind bars, the fewer people he or she is able to victimize.

For those who are concerned with the so-called cruelty of mandatory minimum sentencing in the United States, one might consider the role capital punishment once played in the criminal justice system. For a time, the death penalty was a predetermined minimum sentence for individuals who committed homicide, no matter the circumstances. Arguably, a move toward mandatory minimum sentencing of life imprisonment is more humane than capital punishment. Mandatory minimums keep the public safe from criminals without sentencing them to death.

We can also count on mandatory minimum sentencing to provide us with a sense of certainty about the way the criminal justice system works. Victims and the families of victims know what the sentence is going to be for individuals who are found guilty, even before a sentencing hearing. The same applies to individuals who are convicted. Minimum sentencing can reduce much of the stress for the victims and their families who are awaiting the results.

Finally, individuals facing mandatory minimums may be more likely to provide important information to police

It can be argued that mandatory minimum sentences keep American neighborhoods safer by keeping criminals off the streets.

about their illegal activities in exchange for being allowed to plead guilty to a lesser crime. This gives investigators the leverage they need to indict and convict higher-level criminals, especially in cases involving drug trafficking.

Many people see mandatory minimum sentences as a black and white issue, but there might be a gray area in which there is room for both minimum sentencing and subjective sentencing. A bill called the Justice Safety Valve Act was introduced in Congress in 2017 that would allow judges to have discretion for sentencing in the cases of non-violent, low-risk offenders. Discretion would still not be granted to sex offenders or individuals convicted with violent crimes. This would prevent non-violent offenders from being handed the same sentences as individuals charged with serious violent crimes.

Rather than propose the criminal justice system do away with mandatory minimum sentencing, perhaps opponents of the laws should propose new laws that establish hard guidelines that give judges leeway to deviate from minimum requirements. For instance, perhaps laws could allow a judge to use his or her own discretion if this is the defendant's first offense.

Mandatory minimum sentencing serves a crucial role in the criminal justice system and eliminating this practice would actually harm the current system. With these sentencing guidelines in place, individuals who commit the same crimes will face the same consequences without personal bias.

TEXT-DEPENDENT QUESTIONS

1. What types of offenses are most affected by mandatory minimum sentencing?
2. How might mandatory minimum sentencing affect the actions of the jury?
3. What did the Anti-Drug Abuse Act of 1986 do? How did it impact mandatory minimum sentencing?

RESEARCH PROJECTS

Research your state's stance on mandatory minimum sentencing. What types of offenses does mandatory minimum sentencing handle? What are the possible sentences? How does mandatory minimum sentencing (or lack thereof) in your area impact non-violent crime? What about drug-related crime? Can you find a local case in which an individual received a mandatory minimum sentence as a result of these laws? Write a two-page paper discussing your findings.

WORDS TO UNDERSTAND

deadly force—use of force likely to cause serious bodily injury or death.

imminent—soon to happen.

implicit—implied rather than outwardly expressed.

CAN POLICE AVOID USING DEADLY FORCE?

CHAPTER 5

The use of **deadly force** is an ongoing issue in the criminal justice system. While modern society might commonly associated deadly force with firearms, police officers may also use lethal force in the form of knives, vehicles, explosives, and even their own hands. Any amount of force that can kill another individual is considered lethal, no matter the weapons involved.

When police officers are in high-risk situations, they often only have seconds to make a decision. This sometimes means using lethal force. American police officers participate in about a thousand fatal shootings each year. Officers of the law must make quick decisions in extremely challenging and dangerous situations. Members of the public will later judge those decisions based on their own perceptions.

The law is vague when it comes to defining "excessive force," simply stating that force becomes excessive when officers use more than the force necessary to arrest an individual and to keep the public safe. The public is left to wonder: where is the line between "necessary" and "excessive?" It seems to be a matter of opinion. Still, public opinions differ on how to handle the use of force by police officers. Some people believe that, in most cases, police officers can resolve conflicts or standoffs without using force. Others would argue that using lethal force is necessary to ensure that officers return to their families at the end of their shifts. Finding a solution for the problem at hand may prove more difficult than many believe.

These essays present differing opinions on the use of deadly force by police officers.

Demonstrators in Washington, D.C., march against police shootings and racism.

POLICE OFFICERS CAN AVOID THE USE OF DEADLY FORCE

Incidents involving a police officer's use of deadly force—which often involves shooting a suspect—are often reported in the media. In many of these cases, members of the public claim that deadly force is not always an acceptable option. Some cases have even lead to public protests in the streets and cries for police officers to be charged with homicide. When people are demanding action, how can law enforcement agencies make changes to prevent civilians from dying by lethal force?

One way to curb the use of deadly force by police officers is to revise the policies and guidelines of police departments. Setting safe but clear boundaries for when the use of firearms is permissible would eliminate confusion over whether or not officers are justified in their use of force. Established guidelines would also make it easier to set the standards for reporting the use of excessive force.

California hopes to make changes to legislation to impact the way police officers use deadly force. Lawmakers proposed that police officers only be allowed to use lethal force when a threat of death or serious injury is **imminent**. California police officers would also be required to release information about the shooting to the public. Right now, California has lenient rules surrounding the use of lethal force. New legislation would change this dramatically.

Another common cause for concern is the fact that police officers do have less-than-lethal weapons at their disposal. They often choose not to use these weapons and rather reach for a weapon more likely to be fatal. In 2017, 21-year-old Scout Schultz was shot by a campus police officer at Georgia Tech after calling in a report about a suspicious man with a gun. The officer described Schultz as disoriented and perhaps in the middle of a mental break-down. Evidence suggested that Schultz had a small pocket knife tool but no weapons.

In addressing issues like police brutality, police department administrators should also consider their hiring practices as well. Hiring officers with little self-control and putting them into the field without adequate training may actually encourage the use of deadly force. Changing the types of qualities law enforcement agencies look for is a great place to start.

In fact, expanding the types of police training individuals receive would be beneficial for officers and the communities they serve. **Implicit** bias training might eliminate the fears that often accompany deadly force. Racial issues become increasingly prevalent in studies of bias. One study had subjects respond quickly to a computer simulation involving black and white individuals holding guns and other objects. The study found two race effects, both of which led to black individuals being incorrectly shot more often than innocent white individuals.

Implicit discrimination includes unconscious thoughts. As the study involving shooting innocent and criminal individuals of different races shows, we can assess bias with specific types of testing. Training police officers must involve an assessment of implicit bias and the provision of duties that does not allow one to fall prey to bias.

Many people may argue no racial bias exists in the way police officers use force, but recent studies show that bias does exist. Black people make up 13 percent of America's population, but they still somehow account for 31 percent of those killed by police officers. Addressing bias is not easy, but ongoing training programs may be able to relieve the current tension. Building connections with communities, especially those underserved by police officers, is yet another way to establish trust with those who might otherwise distrust the police.

Additional training for police officers might include relationship-based strategies. Officers can learn better engagement tactics for youthful individuals and those who

Scan here to learn more about the shooting of Michael Brown in Ferguson, Missouri.

A "Stop Murder by Police" protest outside a Los Angeles Police Department station. Historically, the LAPD has had a terrible reputation for racism and brutality.

fall on the LGBT spectrum. Overall better communication with individuals who are English learners or who might not understand local customs would facilitate better experiences between officers and suspects or victims.

Technology can also change the way police officers and the public relate. Barack Obama initiated a program offering body cameras to local police departments. Though the price tag was $75 million, the results may demonstrate their success. In the California town of Rialto, officers began wearing body cams. Two years later, complaints about police officer conduct dropped 88 percent. Along with this decline came a fall in the use of force by officers. Even members of the public changed their behaviors when they realized they were being filmed by the body cameras.

Unfortunately, society must also consider the role of police corruption that accompanies covering up the use of excessive force. If law enforcement communities changed the ways police officers were promoted and worked together, changing the practice of cover-ups is possible. In fact, some law enforcement communities are already doing this. Watts, a neighborhood in Los Angeles, is home to a majority of black and Latino residents. The city has

In recent years, police departments have hired more black or Latino officers, so that the department's racial makeup is more reflective of the communities they serve. This could help to reduce racially motivated incidents in which deadly force is used.

established new guidelines for how police officers must be hired and promoted. The program includes a five-year residency requirement and community evaluation. Other cities, like New Orleans and Tacoma, are also working to facilitate community conversation between civilians and police officers.

 JONATHAN FERRELL

On September 14, 2013, twenty-four-year-old Jonathan Ferrell was driving his vehicle in Charlotte, North Carolina, when he got into an accident. The accident was so bad that Ferrell had to crawl out of the car through a window. Ferrell approached a nearby house and began knocking on the door. A resident inside the home called the police, fearing that someone was trying to break into her home. Officer Randall Kerrick arrived on the scene with two other officers.

When Ferrell saw the officers, he began to run towards them. Some believe Ferrell was relieved to see them, but the officers claimed he was aggressive. Video footage taken from a dashboard camera in one of the police cars does not make clear which story is true. One officer fired a taser at Ferrell, but missed. Kerrick then shot Ferrell ten times. After he died, police found that Ferrell had not been armed.

Finally, ending dangerous high-speed chases and use of lethal weapons would prevent civilian deaths. Sometimes deadly force affects bystanders. This is true for David Perdue, an innocent man attacked by members of the Torrance Police Department while they were searching for Christopher Dorner, a former Los Angeles officer and murderer. The officers involved were afraid for their lives, especially after Dorner had shot several other officers. Police pulled Perdue over to ask him some questions and let him go. Several

Ferrell's family suggested that the shooting was related to Ferrell's race. He was black, whereas Officer Kerrick was white. Prosecutors for the city said that Kerrick did not follow his police training the night he shot Ferrell. Kerrick was charged with voluntary manslaughter, and he was eventually indicted by a grand jury. However, jurors could not agree on whether he was guilty or innocent, and the judge declared a mistrial in the criminal case. Kerrick was not retried. (The city government eventually settled a civil lawsuit over Ferrell's death for $2.25 million.)

Angry at the outcome of Kerrick's trial, protesters demonstrated their frustration in the streets of Charlotte. This has been the case in many situations, prompting protesters to become angry with what they interpret as a lack of justice based on police brutality and racial bias.

moments later, officers rammed his car and shot at him. While they missed, they did drag him out of the car. Perdue and his attorney allege the actions by Torrance officers were completely inexcusable, especially considering the fact that Perdue and Dorner are not even the same race. During the same manhunt, police officers shot through the windows of a pickup truck carrying two women delivering

Some activists are concerned that the increased use of military-style weapons and tactics by police departments contribute to the likelihood that deadly force will be used in encounters.

newspapers. Perdue ended up with a $1.8 million settlement.

High-speed pursuits in police cars have been linked to more than 11,000 deaths since 1979, not counting injuries both minor and serious. In nearly half of all these cases, the victim was not the suspect fleeing but rather a passenger or uninvolved bystander. Most of these pursuits begin as misdemeanors and traffic offenses. Vehicle chases are much more common than police shootings, and the government has recommended law enforcement agencies take action to prevent pursuits as often as possible. For instance, police departments can encourage officers not to make on-the-spot decisions to engage in pursuits without good reason. Police officers need to understand the best times to engage, and perhaps training would prepare them for these possibly deadly decisions.

Finally, law enforcement agencies can discuss the need to focus on non-lethal weapon usage. Bean bag guns and tasers can subdue an individual running away or posing a threat with these weapons, but they are often not the first options officers choose. Do officers feel less confident about these methods? Do other non-lethal but effective options exist? These are questions criminal justice researchers may be able to answer.

While nobody expects cops to be perfect or to act with logic in the face of possible death, the public does have the right to demand that officers be held accountable when they do not use lethal force appropriately.

POLICE MUST BE ALLOWED TO USE DEADLY FORCE

In spite of recent stories decrying the use of deadly force by law enforcement, the truth is that not all force is excessive even if the public deems it so. The case of *Freeman v. Gore* (2007) made permissible the use of force during arrests, warrant service, and detention. Additionally, each state has made their own declarations involving the use of force by police officers. Many cases simply require police officers to use deadly force to protect their communities.

Police officers receive criticism for sometimes shooting suspects while they are fleeing. According to the US

"Enforcement is not the core of our work. Harm reduction, sustaining healthy communities, and work with youth lie at our heart. We must co-produce safety with the community."[17]

—Jim Bueermann, President of The Police Foundation

Non-lethal weapons like this Taser X26 stun gun are not always accurate, and may not subdue an aggressive subject during a dangerous encounter.

Supreme Court ruling in *Tennessee v. Garner* (1985), officers have the right to use deadly force to prevent a suspect from escaping if that suspect poses a significant threat of violence to others. Officers are trained to spot potential threats—training most people outside the force do not have. They are also in more situations that involve risks and intense fear. As a result, they need to make quick decisions, many of which involve using the weapons they have available.

Police officers encounter dangerous situations each day they come in for work. According to FBI statistics, one hundred and eighteen law enforcement professionals were killed in the line of duty in 2016, the most recent year for which complete data is available. While some officers died in accidents, most were killed in confrontations with criminals. The FBI data shows that more than 57,000 police officers were assaulted in 2016. Some were ambushed and attacked, while others were attempting to make arrests or actively investigating cases. It is reasonable to assume that police officers are constantly aware of the potential dangers they face.

In many of the highly publicized police-civilian shooting incidents, police officers had already attempted reasonable alternatives to force, including de-escalation techniques and the use of non-lethal weapons to incapacitate a suspect. Tasers and bean-bag guns are not always accurate, nor do they always function properly. Additionally, officers have limited space in which they can store these items. Officers cannot forego carrying their sidearms in order to carry non-lethal weapons that may not subdue a suspect.

Some people have the idea that police officers can shoot to wound a suspect, without causing a fatal injury. These ideas come from watching too many television shows or movies, in which the hero shoots a gun out of the bad guy's hand before apprehending him. In real life, shootouts are messy, frightening affairs. Police officers, as well as anyone who carries a firearm for self-defense, are taught to aim at a person's center of mass—their chest and torso—to stop a threat. This area is larger and easier to hit than a limb

When police officers must use their service weapon, they are trained to fire at the torso ("center mass") of a person who poses a threat. In a stressful confrontation, it is not easy to hit a person, and the goal is to quickly end the danger to civilians or officers.

Body cameras such as this one can provide video evidence about deadly encounters. However, that evidence can sometimes be inadequate to justify the use of deadly force.

or head, which allows some margin for inaccuracy. After all, in a gunfight people don't stand still like targets on a shooting range, and police must also be aware of others their shots could injure if they miss. Center mass is also where vital organs like the heart and lungs are located, meaning a hit there is more likely to incapacitate an attacker and prevent him from posing a danger to the officer or the public.

The severity of the crime committed contributes to the use of force, especially considering passion and human "heat of the moment" events that occur on the job. A fugitive who is suspected of having committed murder or another serious felony would be considered a serious threat by officers. If officers have reason to believe a suspect who has already committed a serious offense is carrying a weapon, they are trained to not give the suspect an opportunity to use that weapon.

There are ways to deter or prevent the unjustified use of deadly force. Most police departments require officers to use dashboard cameras to record traffic stops and other encounters. A growing number of police departments equip their officers with wearable cameras, which can record their interactions with the public or gather video evidence at crime scenes. These cameras are valuable for providing evidence in court. However, they do not always provide the full context for what happened. After a shooting, the police officer may claim that the victim acted in a threatening or unpredictable way, while the victim's family may claim that he did not. Sometimes, even video evidence can be interpreted differently, depending which side the viewer supports, so questions can remain after reviewing the evidence.

Any time that a police officer must use his or her service weapon, the result is often a devastating tragedy for an American family and community. Unfortunately, many of these instances are simply unavoidable. Police officers tend to every step possible to prevent situations from escalating to a point where they must use deadly force.

TEXT-DEPENDENT QUESTIONS

1. What court case made legal the use of force by police in some instances?
2. What cities are making changes to the ways police officers are hired and promote?
3. What is deadly force? When is deadly force acceptable to use by police officers?

RESEARCH PROJECTS

Research a case in your state involving the use of deadly force by a police officer. Present two sides of the argument. What evidence exists to demonstrate the use of force was necessary? What evidence exists to demonstrate the use of force was not necessary? Then, present your own conclusion. Could anything have prevented the use of force in this scenario?

affidavit—a sworn statement, in writing, that sets out a person's testimony.

affirmative action programs—programs that are intended to improve the educational or employment opportunities of members of minority groups and women.

BCE and CE—alternatives to the traditional Western designation of calendar eras, which used the birth of Jesus as a dividing line. BCE stands for "Before the Common Era," and is equivalent to BC ("Before Christ"). Dates labeled CE, or "Common Era," are equivalent to Anno Domini (AD, or "the Year of Our Lord").

colony—a country or region ruled by another country.

democracy—a country in which the people can vote to choose those who govern them.

discrimination—prejudiced outlook, action, or treatment, often in a negative way.

detention center—a place where people claiming asylum and refugee status are held while their case is investigated.

ethnic cleansing—an attempt to rid a country or region of a particular ethnic group. The term was first used to describe the attempt by Serb nationalists to rid Bosnia of Muslims.

felony—a serious crime; in the United States, a felony is any crime for which the punishment is more than one year in prison or the death penalty.

fundamentalist—beliefs based on a strict biblical or scriptural interpretation of religious law.

median—In statistics, the number that falls in the center of a group, meaning half the numbers are higher than the number and half are lower.

minority—a part of a population different from the majority in some characteristics and often subjected to differential treatment.

paranoia—a mental disorder characterized by the strong belief that the person is being unfairly persecuted.

parole—releasing someone sentenced to prison before the full sentence is served, granted for good behavior.

plaintiff—a person making a complaint in a legal case in civil court.

pro bono—a Latin phrase meaning "for the public good," referring to legal work undertaken without payment or at a reduced fee as a public service.

racial profiling—projecting the characteristics of a few people onto the entire population of a group; for example, when police officers stop people on suspicion of criminal activity solely because of their race.

racism—discrimination against a particular group of people based solely on their racial background.

segregation—the separation or isolation of a race, class, or group from others in society. This can include restricting areas in which members of the race, class, or group can live; placing barriers to social interaction; separate educational facilities; or other discriminatory means.

FURTHER READING

Alexander, Michelle. *The New Jim Crow: Mass Incarceration in the Age of Colorblindness*. New York: The New Press, 2010.

Bernstein, Nell. *Burning Down the House: The End of Juvenile Prison*. New York: The New Press, 2014.

Bonner, Raymond. *Anatomy of Injustice*. New York: Vintage Books, 2012.

Day O'Connor, Sandra. *The Majesty of the Law: Reflections of a Supreme Court Justice*. New York: Random House, 2003.

Duane, James. *You Have the Right to Remain Innocent*. New York: Little A, 2016.

Feld, Barry. *Bad Kids: Race and the Transformation of the Juvenile Court*. New York: Oxford University Press, 1999.

Forest, Stuart. *Down, Out, and Under Arrest: Policing and Everyday Life in Skid Row*. Chicago: University of Chicago Press, 2016.

Foucault, Michel. *Discipline and Punishment: The Birth of Prison*. New York: Vintage Books, 1974.

Kerman, Piper. *Orange Is the New Black: My Year in a Women's Prison*. New York: Spiegel & Grau, 2010.

Loevy, Robert *The Civil Rights Act of 1964: The Passage of the Law that Ended Racial Segregation*. New York: State University of New York Press, 1997.

Morton, Michael. *Getting Life*. New York: Simon & Schuster, 2015.

Petersilia, Joan. *When Prisoners Come Home: Parole and Prisoner Reentry*. New York: Oxford University Press, 2003.

Reiman, Jeffrey. *The Rich Get Richer and the Poor Get Prison: Ideology, Class, and Criminal Justice*. Boston: Pearson/Allyn & Bacon, 2007.

Stone, Vali. *Cops Don't Cry: A Book of Help and Hope for Police Families*. Ontario: Creative Bound, Inc, 1999.

Tonry, Michael. *Punishing Race: A Continuing American Dilemma*. New York: Oxford University Press, 2012.

Toobin, Jeffrey. *The Run of His Life: The People v. O. J. Simpson*. New York: Random House, 1996.

INTERNET RESOURCES

https://www.theguardian.com/us-news/ng-interactive/2015/jun/01/the-counted-police-killings-us-database
A detailed database maintained by *The Guardian* newspaper that provides information about people killed by police officers.

https://inequality.stanford.edu/publications/media/details/searching-work-criminal-record
Watch this video to learn more about the challenges individuals face when they try to find work after leaving prison.

https://www.penalreform.org/wp-content/uploads/2018/04/PRI_Global-Prison-Trends-2018_EN_WEB.pdf
This report discusses criminal justice trends, specifically regarding imprisonment and crime rates.

https://www.prisonpolicy.org/reports/pie2018.html
This graphic provides a visual and analytical breakdown of America's prison system as it stands today.

https://centerforprisonreform.org/wp-content/uploads/2015/09/Diversion-Programs-Cover.png
Is jail the only solution? This report analyzes a variety of diversion programs that might be more effective than imprisonment for non-violent offenders.

https://www.aclu.org/sites/default/files/field_document/aclu_bullies_in_blue_4_11_17_final.pdf
Is school policing a good idea? This report takes a look at the impact of campus police officers on students, especially racial minorities.

https://drivingwhileblacknashville.files.wordpress.com/2016/10/driving-while-black-gideons-army.pdf
This report on racial discrimination in traffic stops may shed some light on police practice in Nashville.

www.americanbar.org/groups/criminal_justice/resources/case_updates.html
Keep up to date with ongoing Supreme Court cases in America. This website offers case summaries, outcomes, and updates for each term.

http://www.urban.org/UploadedPDF/311156_Does_Parole_Work.pdf
This report explores the impact of parole for inmates released back into society, analyzing whether these programs are successful in preventing recidivism and protecting public safety.

CHAPTER NOTES

[1] Linda Deutsch, "OJ Simpson Murder Trial: 'If it Doesn't Fit, You Must Acquit,' NBC Los Angeles (June 11, 2014). https://www.nbclosangeles.com/news/local/OJ-Simpson-20-Years-Later-Glove-Fit-Darden-Dunne-Murder-Trial-of-the-Century-262534821.html

[2] John Adams, argument for the defense in the trial of William Wemms, James Hartegan, William M'Cauley, [and others] ... for the Murder of Crispus Attucks, [and others], ... Superior Court of Judicature, Court of Assize, and General Goal Delivery ... taken in Short-Hand by John Hodgson, Boston, 1770. https://founders.archives.gov/documents/Adams/05-03-02-0001-0004-0016#LJA03d031n1

[3] The Constitution of the United States, Amendment 4. https://www.constituteproject.org/constitution/United_States_of_America_1992

[4] Barack Obama, "Remarks by the President at the Annual NAACP Convention," July 15, 2015. https://www.naacp.org/latest/remarks-by-the-president-at-the-naacp-annual-convention/

[5] Inimai Chettiar, quoted in Jeremy Travis, "The Growth of Incarceration in the United States: Exploring Causes and Consequences," National Research Council (2014), p. 40.

[6] Hillary Clinton, keynote speech on criminal justice at the David N. Dinkins Leadership and Public Policy Forum, Columbia University, April 29, 2015. https://internal.sipa.columbia.edu/news-center/video/hillary-rodham-clinton-speaks-on-race-justice

[7] Associated Press, "Gov. Signs Bill Adding 53,000 Prison Beds," *Press-Telegram* (May 2007). https://www.presstelegram.com/2007/05/03/gov-signs-bill-adding-53000-prison-beds/

[8] ibid.

[9] National Institute of Justice, "Indigent Defense." https://www.nij.gov/topics/courts/indigent-defense/Pages/welcome.aspx

[10] "The Challenges of Prisoner Re-Entry Into Society," Simmons School of Social Work (July 12, 2016). https://socialwork.simmons.edu/blog/Prisoner-Reentry/

[11] Steve Rose, "*Strong Island*'s Yance Ford: 'I have no interest in giving my brother's killer any space in this film'," *The Guardian* (September 2017). https://www.theguardian.com/film/2017/sep/13/strong-islands-yance-ford-i-have-no-interest-in-giving-my-brothers-killer-any-space-in-this-film

[12] Aswad Thomas, quoted in "Reducing Crime and Incarceration," Public Welfare Foundation (January 17, 2017). http://www.publicwelfare.org/reducing-crime-and-incarceration/

[13] Samuel R. Gross et al, "Race and Wrongful Convictions in the United States," National Registry of Exonerations (March 7, 2017), pp. 26–27. http://www.law.umich.edu/special/exoneration/Documents/Race_and_Wrongful_Convictions.pdf

[14] ibid, p. 28.

[15] Barack Obama, "Statement by the President," The White House (August 18, 2014). https://obamawhitehouse.archives.gov/the-press-office/2014/08/18/statement-president

[16] Marc Mauer, "The Impact of Mandatory Sentencing Policies in the United States," testimony before the Canadian Senate Standing Committee on Legal and Constitutional Affairs (October 28, 2009). https://www.sencanada.ca/Content/SEN/Committee/402/lega/pdf/17issue.pdf

[17] Jim Bueermann, quoted in John A. Calhoun, "Building Trust Between Police and the Communities They Serve," National League of Cities (November 20, 2016). https://www.nlc.org/article/building-trust-between-police-and-the-communities-they-serve

ORGANIZATIONS TO CONTACT

The Dream Corps
436 14th St., Suite 920
Oakland, CA 94612
Email: nisha@dreamcorps.us
Website: https://www.thedreamcorps.org

Families Against Mandatory Minimums
1612 K Street NW, Suite 700
Washington, DC 20006
Phone: 202-822-6700
Website: https://famm.org/

Legal Services for Prisoners with Children
1540 Market St., Suite 490
San Francisco, CA 94102
Phone: (415) 255-7036
Fax: (415) 552-3150
Website: www.prisonerswithchildren.org/

MacArthur Foundation
Office of Grants Management
140 S. Dearborn Street
Chicago, IL 60603-5285
Phone: (312) 726-8000
Email: 4answers@macfound.org
Website: https://www.macfound.org/
programs/criminal-justice/

The Marshall Project
156 West 56th Street, Suite 701
New York, NY 10019
Phone: (212) 803-5200
Email: info@themarshallproject.org
Website:www.themarshallproject.org/

The National Institute for Criminal
Justice Reform
Email: info@nicjr.org
Website: http://nicjr.org/

Prison Fellowship
44180 Riverside Parkway
Lansdowne, VA 20176
Phone: 1-800-206-9764
Email: info@pfm.org
Website: www.prisonfellowship.org

Prison University Project
PO Box 492
San Quentin, CA 94964
Phone: (415) 455-8088
Email: info@prisonuniversityproject.org
Website: prisonuniversityproject.org/

Right on Crime
901 Congress Avenue
Austin, TX 78701
Phone: (512) 472-2700
Email: roc@texaspolicy.com
Website: http://rightoncrime.com/

The Sentencing Project
1705 DeSales St, NW, 8th Floor
Washington, D.C. 20036
Phone: (202) 628-0871
Fax: (202) 628-1091
Email: staff@sentencingproject.org
Website: www.sentencingproject.org/

Vera Institute of Justice
233 Broadway, 12th Floor
New York, NY 10279
Phone: (212) 334-1300
Website: https://www.vera.org/

INDEX

INDEX

AUTHOR'S BIOGRAPHY AND CREDITS

ABOUT THE AUTHOR

Ashley Nicole is an author and true crime writer with a background in psychology and sociology. Though a California native, she currently lives in Arizona, where she enjoys hiding from the sun and writing novels.

PICTURE CREDITS